Chaotic Beauty

(Poems of Love, Loss, Heartbreak and the
Human Experience)

Leslie James

BookLeaf Publishing

Presentation by *BookLeaf Publishing*

Web: www.bookleafpub.com

E-mail: info@bookleafpub.com

ISBN: 9789358312225

First edition 2023

I dedicate this book to My mother Gwendolyn James, my Grandmother Tempie Lee James, Grandfather Clarence James and my Aunt Helen Beal, My Uncle Donald James, Mollie Toon, Darlene Dennis and Share Bear. Thank you and I love you all!

ACKNOWLEDGEMENT

First and foremost I thank God because without him none of this would be possible. I want to thank BookLeaf Publishing for giving me the opportunity to have my first book of poetry published. I'd like to thank Eber & Wein Publishing, for being the very first publisher. I would like to thank my Mother Gwendolyn James for her unwavering love and support. Thank you for believing in me and always having my back. Without you I would not have come this far. I'd like to take Mollie Toon for always being a cheerleader for my writing. Believing I was good enough and pushing me to get published, because without her I wouldn't have known of this writing challenge or this publishing opportunity. I would like to thank my Grandmother Tempie Lee James, Grandfather Clarence James and my Aunt Helen Beal and Uncle Donald James for loving and believing in me too. Thank you too the rest of my family for loving me as well. I would also like to thank Darlene Dennis for believing in me and my writing and pushing me to get published.

PREFACE

Most of these poems are written about my own life experiences. A few are written through the eyes of friends and loved ones. All of it is my original poetry.

Mother

Mother, you are the butterfly,
Beautiful and unique
Your smile has warmed
So many hearts
Your arms they've sheltered me

Mother, you have been
My guardian angel
Always seeing me through
Loving me no matter what
And believing in me too

Mother, you are like the sunshine,
You light so many lives
And though you may not know it
You are loved a thousand times

Thank You

We used to look at rainbows,
The beautiful colors that fill the sky
You told me if I spread my wings
One day I'd learn to fly

You've been my inspiration for
Which helped me make it through
Everything that I have learned
I've learned it all from you

You thought me to be strong,
Even if it looked like I could not go on

You told me if I wanted something bad enough
I could make it come true
I look at who I am today and
I owe it all to you

My Mystery Love

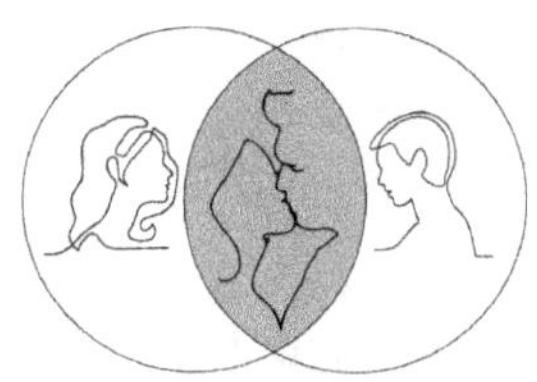

You walk towards me
Through the darkness
And caress my cheek;

The softest touch

You stand close;
I can feel the warmth
Radiating from your skin
Electricity flows through my body and
My heart races
As I anticipate the most sensual kiss
I can smell your breath: so sweet
Your lips touch mine
I close my eyes
My knees begin to buckle
You pull me closer

Holding me against your body
The kiss becoming
So fierce and so intense
Our hearts beat in sync
Racing faster and faster
I can feel your muscles
Every ripple of your body
As you hold me in your arms
Wanting you so badly
But needing you even more
And as suddenly as it began, it ends;

Your mouth leaves mine.
I feel your warm breath in my ear
As you whisper the words,
"I Love you. Goodbye, my love."
I open my eyes; you are gone
Nowhere in sight
I call out to you
But no one answers
I look for you to no avail
I sit down on the bed, wondering
Did this happen?
Were you here?
Is it possible that I imagined this?
And the most painful thought
Crosses my mind
Could the most passionate kiss
I had ever felt in my entire life

Have just been a fantasy
Then at that moment;
I lick my lips
I can still taste you there;
So sweet
And it was at that moment that I knew
You had been real
That's when I feel the cool night air
Coming in through the open window
I walk over and look out at the moon
And the stars in the sky
I look down and notice a single red rose
lying on the windowsill, I pick it up and
take in the aromatic rosy scent
I then hear footsteps below
And look down to see someone fleeing into the
night
I lean out and whisper
Into the darkness
I love you too,
Goodbye, my mystery love

The Satisfied Lover

I hunger for your body
I thirst for your soul
Passions erupting
Emotions unfold

The taste of your mouth
The smell of your skin
The warmth of your touch
We deliciously sin

Lost in a moment
Entangled in lust
Our bodies intertwined
In a climatic rush

Immense satisfaction
You're still holding me tight
As we bask in the glow
Of our passionate night

Accept Me

Love me,
Touch me,
Taste me,
Feel me,
Just be with me;

Breathe me,
Kiss me,
Hold me,
make love to me,
Just stay with me;

Please me,
Tease me,
Pleasure me,
Just come and lay with me;

Read me,
Know me,
Understand me,
Just accept me;

Hazel Eyes

Can you tell me why those hazel eyes
Always see right through me
Deep into my soul
What no one knows
That thing that drew you to me
Can you tell me why
I look into those same eyes
And can never tell what you're thinking
I get lost in a sea of brown and green
I can't breathe
but I can't stop drinking
I thirst to know
What's in your soul
What drives you and keeps you going
What makes your heart break
And what makes you ache
For me, in the
early morning

The Great Divide

Look into my eyes,
See the questions deep inside.
See the pain that tears at my heart,
Feel the sorrow that drowns me.

Tell me that you'll never leave,
Tell me that you'll stay,
Tell me all the reasons why,
It's in my bed you lay.

I feel your arms around me,
But I still have to know,
If you found somebody new,
Would you let me go?

You tell me that you need me,
And I'm the only one.
You tell me that I have your heart,
And that you'll never run.

Yet, you keep things bottled up inside and
You won't say what you feel.
So, how do we make this work,
If you can't keep it real

I lay on my side of the bed at night,
And cry myself to sleep.
And when you think no one is listening,
Sometimes I hear you weep.

You ask me to be honest with you,
But I don't think it's fair,
For you to ask me to do something,
That you refuse to share.

It hurts to think that you don't trust me,
With what is bothering you.
But I can't help you get past the pain,
If you don't let me through.

So open up your heart,
And let me see inside.
Let me see what I can do,
To help close this great divide.

Remember Me

Dark clouds move in; the thunder rolls
It's dark outside, black as my soul
You took my heart with you that fateful day
You left this world and floated away
The tears I cry cannot compare
To the pain I have inside to bear

As I lie awake in bed at night
The memories of you come rushing back with a
bite
Of pain so real I hate to think
There will always be that missing link

I should have known some months before
When you came knocking at my door
With that anguished look in your eyes;
Your broken smile made me want to cry

I did know then, but I was scared
Of the connection that we shared
I should have never let you go
But I could never let you know
How much I truly loved you so

There were so many obstacles
That was standing in our way
We left so many stones unturned
And so much left to say

I wish I could have one more day
So I could see you smile
hold your hand, tell you I was wrong
And I'll see you in a while

I'm so sorry it took this tragedy
To truly make me see
And now all I can do is pray;
that you'll remember me.

Unrequited Love

She is beautiful on the outside,
But ugliness radiates from within
From the darkness of her soul
An unrequited love avenged

What a pity it is to learn
A love given is not a love returned
To find your heart is all alone
Will turn your heart to the blackest stone

For she, it seems, cannot find
A love untainted and divine
So, she will take revenge on he
Who loves another over she

And he will die the blackest death
At his unrequited lover's blade, he'll rest

And he will know that it was she
Who turned his lover's blade on he

What Could Have Been

It has been asked of me a thousand times,
If I have any regrets
And a thousand times I replied
I can't think of any yet
But if I'm honest with myself
I can think of more than one
And the one that could have been
Is the biggest one
I think about his smile and
How good he was to me
And I wish that I could find a way to turn
What could have been into what could still be
I hold the memories of him fondly in my heart
And wonder if we ever met again could we have
a fresh start

I promise this time things will be so different
As I was much too young then and not ready for
a commitment
But I am older now. I believe I am wiser
And I will make him this promise when I look
into his eyes
That I will try my hardest to be the woman he
needs,
And I hope that he will let me show him how
much to me he truly means

Beautiful Ghost

I fell in love with a man I can only describe as a
beautiful ghost.
He flickered into my life in the beat of a heart,
and was gone in a flicker of the next beat
The most puissant powerful beat and
though it only lasted a moment
it has now become my lifelong obsession

Many Pieces

I'm sad but no one knows it
I cry but no one hears
In my room when I'm alone
I cry these only tears

My heart's in many pieces
My soul is shattered too
Can you tell me what is that
I'm supposed to do
To keep from missing you

You told me you'd never
Break my heart
You promised you'd never lie
But now it seems all I ever do
is sit alone and cry.

You told me that you loved me
You used to seem to care
Now every time I turn around
You're not even there

I would have done anything
To keep you in my life
But you got up and walked out the door

And didn't even say goodbye
Well, now you know my heart's in many pieces
And my soul is shattered too,
But even though you've done me wrong
I'll go on loving you

Falling

She sits in a dark room
The rain begins to beat down
Like little men with tiny hammers
Beating on a tin roof
The room starts to spin
all she can see
is herself falling
And then she hits
And that's it
That's the end;
She's gone

A Good Recipe

Though I may not always like you
I will love you always
Stand by your side
And walk through this life with you
That is love
We will be honest with one another
Always faithful and true
Can tell each other when the other is out of line
Only ever wanting what is best for the other
And knowing that we can depend on
Each other to be truthful and fair
That is trust
Though we do not always agree
We talk about it, compromise

Meet in the middle
And come to an understanding
That is called communication
I will not always be right
I know that and admit when I am wrong
You will not always be right
You know that and admit when you are wrong
We accept our faults,
realize it doesn't matter who's right or wrong
What matters is that we respect each other's
opinions
Listen to what each other has to say
Think it over and either agree or
Agree to disagree
That is respect
Love, Communication, truth, and Respect
Four ingredients to any good relationship.
There is a fifth ingredient
Which is the most important
It should always come first
A relationship with God
God is where it should start and where it should
end.
When you have the first four ingredients
You have the recipe for a good relationship
When you start with the fifth
And put your relationship with God first and
foremost
You have a good recipe for a good marriage.

Love of A Brother

Caught in the middle
Stuck in between
Love and happiness
Hurt and pain
Arms so warm and inviting
Eyes so cold a love dividing
Peace, on the one hand
Heartache in the other
Which one do I choose
The love of a brother
Like ice and fire
Like day and night
All choices wrong
No choice is right
No matter what I choose

There will inevitably be a fight
Following my heart
Will start the war
Despite what I feel
There could never be more
Because either lover
Will break the heart of a brother

Stressed

I love you deeply; though
You continue to stress me out.
All of your complaining and nitpicking,
Your words and
The negativity you bring about
Are making me crazy and
I want to scream and shout.
I never tell you,
Because that is who I am.
The one who cares more about others' feelings,

then the pain that I'm in

emotionally or physically,
I continue to stuff it down.
Even though I'm breaking inside,

I do not make a sound.
I shed a tear now and then,
When you can not see;
Because it is all about you
And not about me

Grief

As time goes by, you wonder
What is the point of holding on,
Because eventually, it all gets snatched away
Death comes no matter what
And there is nothing we can do or say
The pain is sharp and crushing
You feel like you can not breathe
Because you will never see that person again
Except maybe in a picture or in your dreams
Or the memories that you clutch close to your
heart
You cry until you have no more tears left
And the memories are just too hard
Though they are good
Missing the person begins to tear your soul apart
You never thought you'd see them weak

You thought they'd always be strong
Because you saw them as a superhero
When it turns out they were only human like the
rest of us all along
You know that someday someone will be hurt
from missing you
And you wish that no one would ever again
Have to feel the way that you do.

To My Grandpa

You left this world when I was not yet ten years
old.
It hurt so bad to lose the only dad I'd ever
known.
I didn't know then how much it would affect me
or how much you truly meant in my life.
You stepped in and took over the role as my dad
when my bio dad couldn't even be bothered to
play the part.
We share many precious memories that will live
on forever in my heart.
When I think about you and how much I truly
lost,
my eyes become a well of tears until the tears
spill down my cheeks,
and I can not contain the grief of what you're
missing presence cost.
No, I am not blaming you, and I am not blaming
me;
I am not blaming anyone; I only wish it had not
taken me this long to see
that you were my dad, at least in any way that
mattered.
You loved me, protected me, and taught me to be
good.

You were a wonderful Grandpa and Dad from
where I stood.
I didn't realize until now that you were the dad
I always looked for; but couldn't see I already
had.
I wish we could have had longer and that we
could have talked when I got older.
Maybe we would have shared some funny
stories;
Maybe we would have laughed.
I will never know, but I will cherish all of the
memories that we had,
And I will always love you and think of you as
my dad.

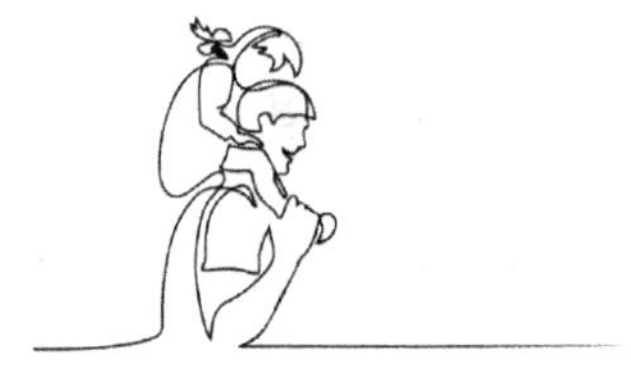

A Whisper in the Night

You came in through my window last night
And whispered in my ear
You told me that you love me
And that you will always be near
You told me that
You brought me roses
And left them on my desk
And wrote a song about an angel
Whose love was so selfless

You told me that the angel
that you wrote about was me
And that when we were together
I made you feel so free

You told me that you visited me before
And watched me sleep
And that I called your name
And softly began to weep

You came over to my bedside
and told me not to cry
and that one day we'll be together,
Dancing in the Sky

Doomed

Violent memories
Of a love gone wrong
Our passions ran deep
But our anger held strong

Our words cut deep;
Like a knife through the heart
Fighting in vain;
For this love doomed from the start

Angel in the Snow

There was a time when I would run and cower in
the shade
but you took my hand and guided me, told me
not to be afraid
You taught me how to smile again.
You taught me to be me.
You taught me that, like an eagle that soars high
above the trees
I could learn to spread my wings.
You taught me to be free.

You helped me in so many ways.
You may not even know,
but because of you, I learned to fly
Like an angel in the snow

You showed me how to love again.
You opened up my heart.
Every word you spoke was like an angel playing
his harp.
There's no one in this world that I would prefer
to love or know
than you, as beautiful as heaven
Like an angel in the snow